The Buzz About *Simon Says*

"In the past 10 years, I have watched with great joy and pride the development of Simon's heart, soul, character and dreams. Few people have the clarity of thinking and the tenacity to figure out who they are and then to pursue their dreams regardless of the obstacles. Simon should be the poster child for this process. He is a loyal friend, an encourager, and a man of faith. Read this book and find what makes him tick!"

Larry Kreider, President, The Gathering USA

"Simon has hit the nail on the head. This book will change your life."

Ann Brown-Payne, President, The Alliance

"This book is a great tool for those who wish to rekindle their passion and spirit."

Sean Mahoney, Ft. Lauderdale, Florida

"Absolutely sensational! I have read your book twice so far and will read it at least once more."

Cheryl Alker, Houston, Texas

"I loved this book! It's FULL of encouragement and Simon's spirit of energy is on every page!"

Mary Tomlinson, Windermere, Florida

"After hearing Simon speak, attending his workshop, and reading this book, I have truly been inspired! I've laughed and cried and now I'm ready to look at my life from a whole new perspective."

Jennifer Clay, San Jose, California

Mel,
Go for IT!

Simon Says...Dream
Live a Passionate Life!

Simon

By Simon T. Bailey

Foreword - Mark Chironna

Infinite Possibilities Publishing Group, Inc.
Florida

Most IP Books are available at special quantity discounts for bulk pur-
chases for sales promotions, premiums, fundraising, or educational use.

For details, write: Special Markets, IP Publishing Group, PO Box 150823
Altamonte Springs, FL 32715-0823
Email: IPpublishingGrp@aol.com

IP Books
Published by Infinite Possibilities Publishing Group, Inc.
PO Box 150823
Altamonte Springs, FL 32715-0823
Email: IPpublishingGrp@aol.com
Website: www.IPpublishingOnline.com

Cover and text layout by:
Rachelle Harris, Designs by Rachelle
www.designsbyrachelle.com

Cover Design by:
Wanda Alexander/Panache

Library of Congress Control Number: 2003107483

ISBN#: 0-9729912-0-4

Printed in the United States of America

10 9 8 7 6 5 4

TABLE OF CONTENTS

CHAPTERS

Dedication

Reneé, my wife, you are the best thing that ever happened to me. Thanks for believing in me and pushing me to be all that I could possibly be. The best is yet to come.

Daniel, you are my hero. Daddy loves you. Remember who you are; you are more than what you've become.

Madison, you are Daddy's beautiful angel. You complete my life. Every time I look into your eyes, I realize just how blessed I am.

Acknowledgements

First of all, thanks to my heavenly father, maker of the universe and creator of all things.

To my parents and in-laws, thanks for your patience and prayers. I love you.

To my spiritual father, and life coach, Dr. Mark Chironna, thank you for modeling for me integrity, authenticity and wisdom.

To my editors, The Institute For Successful Leadership, Inc. (Tremene Triplett and Sherice Brocknbrough) and MindLeap (Steve Klodt), you are awesome. Thanks for stretching and pulling out of me the simplistic nuggets of truth that will forever impact generations to come.

To my publisher, Shelley Parris, you are incredible. Thanks for helping me see the infinite possibilities in my writing.

To my clothing designer, Auke Hempenius, the man, the myth, the legend. You are destined to be one of the greatest clothing brands in the 21st century.

To graphic artist, Wanda Alexander, thank you for your patience and creative design.

To the Walt Disney World® Resort, thank you for all of the character-building moments.

Introduction

When I was fourteen and growing up in Buffalo, New York, I had a dream one night that I was flying higher and higher, and everything within me was soaring higher and higher. Something inside of me kept me looking up, and the more I looked up the higher I went. I was afraid if I looked down I would fall. All I could do was put my trust in God and believe that everything in front of me was connected to my greater purpose.

The objective of this book is to demonstrate the flight path of transitioning from dream to reality. Each chapter is a step forward toward the future that awaits all of us. By joining me on this journey, you will discover the vast amount of wealth that exists inside of you, recognize your dream, and improve your life.

At the end of each chapter there is a journal page for you to write the steps that you will take to live a passionate life. I invite you to write down what you are learning from each chapter and review your notes prior to starting your day and prior to going to sleep.

Each chapter will immerse you in thought. Thinking about your life in a brand new way and writing in your journal will capture what is most alive in you.

You'll see why either looking back or looking down is not an option for you. The journey is onward and upward. My friends strap on your courage and let's take flight.

Your life will never be the same again after you read this book. You can no longer sit in a comfortable position and watch your life pass you by. I wrote this book so that the volcano of destiny would erupt from the depths of your being. My spirit gave birth to this book to push you in the direction of your destiny. Once you digest the intent behind the content, open your heart and mind to make decisions that will move you toward an incredible future.

Simon says, "Your best days are in front of you and everything that you've experienced up to this point has prepared you to appreciate true success. Never give up, never look back—the best view is right in front of you."

Passion is essential for the human spirit. If you are enthused about living a fulfilled life, then settling for mediocrity is out of the question. This book is a tool that will reveal additional options available to you when you decide to win consistently. You are standing at the cliff of possibility, calculating the probability of chance, while being nudged by the wind of opportunity. What are you waiting for? Go for it. This is the moment that you've been waiting for. MOVE.

The following quote inspired me to find my passion.

"Our deepest fear is that we are powerful beyond measure. It is light, not our darkness that most frightens us. We ask ourselves, who am I to be brilliant, gorgeous, talented and fabulous? Actually, who are you not to be? You are a child of God. Your playing small doesn't serve the world. There's nothing enlightened about shrinking so that other people won't feel insecure around you. We were born to make manifest the glory of God that is within us. It's not just in some of us; it's in everyone. And as we let our own light shine we unconsciously give other people permission to do the same. As we are liberated from our own fear, our presence automatically liberates others."

- Nelson Mandela

Foreword

As long as humanity has been on the planet, dreams have lived within the human heart. The ancients believed that dreams were a vital part of experiencing personal renewal and the healing of one's life. Living a life of passion requires waking up and living out the dream that lives inside you. Simon Bailey is a dream specialist. He has lived with his own dream from the time he was a child and has refined it, studied it, embraced it, honored it, and worked it. Now it is becoming a living reality and is bringing others into aliveness when he speaks. Simon really does speak to you. When Simon "says" dream, he gives you the tools to do so. When Simon "says" that first class is the only option, he actually shows you how to book the flight of the dream of your life in preferred seating. Take the time to learn from a lifelong learner, who is well on his way to being one of the key voices of the new millennium to inspire and instruct a generation that is ready to make the most of its time on the planet. If you thought you lost your passion, you'll have it back within the first few pages of this book you now hold in your hands. If you misdirected your passion, have no fears, he will show you how to get yourself back on track. If you are not sure what your passion is, there is much here to help clarify your own unique purpose to empower you to become all you were meant to be. Simon Bailey will awaken you to the potential inside you and show you how to turn it into actual experience and fulfillment. When you discover that the dream inside you will actually bring you into wholeness and well-being, you'll decide it is worth the investment in your future to live as passionately as possible. When Simon says, "dream," he gives you all the resources you need to do so and then some. Now that you hold the key in your hand, unlock the door of your mind and heart, and let Simon lead you into your desired future.

Mark J. Chironna, Ph.D.

CHAPTER ONE

Simon Says, "Wake Up"

"If you love what you do, you will never work a day in your life."

-Ron Rubin

It was a beautiful spring morning, and I was beginning a vacation of ten days, something that is rare for me. I had an epiphany at 9:41 A.M. that day. It deeply impacted my personal philosophy and left me speechless for a few minutes. Here is what I discovered for myself. LIFE WAS NOT MEANT TO BE LIVED IN THE RAT RACE. I didn't create the rat race, but everything that I had achieved up to this point was the result of climbing the corporate ladder to find new and better cheese...so I thought. Once I got to the midpoint of my professional career, what financial investment counselors call the wealth-building years (30-40 years old), I realized that my ladder was against the wrong wall. Here I was at age 34, unhappy, unfulfilled, disappointed that I had not accomplished more with my life. I was simply going through the motions, attending meetings, calling the shots, cutting deals, hiring, redeploying, and firing, if necessary. My EGO was out of control.

At one point, I believed the success of my people, my race, was riding on my shoulders, and if I spoke articulately and used my charming personality, then others in a position of influence would support me and promote me through the system. *Why* should they support me? Well, in my mind it was the right thing to do. It would show other people that they supported the diversity movement. I thought that's what I wanted. So, I was smiling on the outside but dying on the inside for my cheese-chasing ways. What was I doing? What was I thinking? Chasing after more cheese was more about me trying to impress others instead understanding my purpose for existence. I was acting as if I had my act together, but I had yet to make an impact.

December 10, 2001, Mike Vogel, a freelance writer for *Florida Trend* magazine interviewed me for an upcoming full-page feature story about trendsetters in Florida. During this interview, he asked me where I saw myself ten to fifteen years from now? Amazingly, I said, "I see myself as president of Walt Disney World® Resort some day and chairman and

CEO of the Walt Disney Company." The day the magazine hit the newsstands in February 2002, it featured my story on page 12, and when I read the story, my statement finally hit me like a pile of bricks. What in the world was I thinking? I wasn't passionate about becoming the number one guy at Disney. I was simply trying to position myself in the eyes of my superiors as someone to consider for the next big promotion. This was a strategic move, I thought, and I believed that it would help move my career along faster and it would launch my internal political campaign for an executive promotion. Did it? What do you think? Of course not! I learned a valuable lesson about myself, however. Effective leaders serve for the good of all humanity instead of being self-serving. In other words, my entire professional career was based on the need to perform and impress others, and the truth is that I didn't even know who I was! I simply was pursuing a promotion to obtain more green cheese (paycheck), meanwhile decaying on the inside.

On December 31, 2002, I was reading the last chapter of *Wild at Heart*, written by John Eldredge, and he shared the following insight from his spiritual mentor Gil Bailie: *"Don't ask yourself what the world needs. Ask yourself what makes you come alive, and go do that, because what the world needs is people who have come alive."* Well, after reading this, it felt as if Fourth of July fireworks were shooting through my veins. I knew that Bailie was speaking directly to me. I realized that I no longer loved my job. I was doing what I *had* to do instead of doing what I *wanted* to do.

On the day of my epiphany I was in a local hangout for early risers who enjoy good coffee, pastries, bagels, *USA Today*, and a friendly chat with a stranger. As I walked in I noticed two gentlemen sitting in the corner wearing golf shirts, sipping a cup of coffee, and enjoying life. Then I noticed another group of people slowly chatting, enjoying the classical music, and laughing; soaking up the peaceful atmosphere of a beautiful spring day. Each person that I saw appeared to be stress-free, on top of the world, and passionate about living life by design instead of punching a timecard for another ten-hour professional adventure! It was on this day that I realized that there were people who had taken a different path, left the rat race either through choice or retirement and now were creating new chapters in their lives.

It's Just a Job

What is amazing to me about this entire scenario is that normally, at 10:00 A.M. on most weekdays, I would have just concluded a meeting and would have jumped into my car to drive to another one! After the meeting, I would have returned to my desk by noon and begun responding to fifty E-mails from people needing an instant answer. This is a normal routine for some people who endure the bottleneck of an E-mail universe.

But that day, while waiting in line to order my bagel, I realized that there were people who were not constantly reading E-mails, not stuck responding to instant messages on their PDAs, not sitting in rush hour traffic, and not multi-tasking their lives away! There has to be more to life than just sitting in meetings and responding to E-mails! How many times have you said to yourself, "Is this all life has to offer me?" Don't we deserve more than working a job, paying taxes, paying bills and running errands? Every day we wake up to chase goals we think we want without asking ourselves if the goals truly fulfill ourselves. For some people the chase itself is what it's all about. But are these people mastering the chase or is the chase mastering them? Robert Kiyosaki, author of *Rich Dad Poor Dad*, said this, "Your future is what you do today, regardless of your dreams."

Talk to Yourself

As I got closer to ordering my bagel, a light bulb in my head clicked on. I said to myself, "Simon you are the sum total of everything that you think, do, say and feel! *You have attracted to your life what you are!* You are where you are today because of what you think, do, say, and by God's divine plan." When was the last time you had a heart-to-heart conversation with yourself? When was the last time you asked yourself these transformational questions?

- Where have I been?
- Where am I going?
- What am I most passionate about?
- What do I really, really, really, really want out of life?

Po Bronson said this in his book *What Should I Do with My Life?:* "Most people have good instincts about where they belong but make poor choices and waste productive years on the wrong work." He also shares a story about Joe Olchefske, who, one night, riding up the elevator of his apartment building, met the newly hired Seattle Schools Superintendent John Stanford. Soon after, Stanford offered Olchesfske the CFO job to help him in turning around the troubled school system. Olchefske accepted. Stanford rallied the city around school reform and earned the nickname Prophet of Hope.

Meanwhile, Olchefske slashed millions from the budget and bloodlessly fired principals, never allowing his passions to interfere with decisions. People called him Prophet of Doom. Then Stanford died suddenly of leukemia. It was one of the great crises in the city's history. Who could fill this void? Certainly not the green-eyeshaded CFO. But Stanford's death transformed Olchefske. It broke him open, and he discovered in himself a new ability to connect with people emotionally, not just rationally. As the new superintendent, he draws on that gift. He puts up with a lot of bureaucrap, but he says that avoiding crap shouldn't be the objective in finding the right work. The right question is, How can I find my something that moves my heart, so that the inevitable crap storm is bearable?

Channeling Energy

Passion is one of the most important words in the twenty-first century! Are you pursuing your passion or are you taking up space on Earth by inhaling free oxygen? When you identify your passion, you also will discover a variety of options that are available to you. Now, I am not telling you to quit your job or to move to California in pursuit of becoming an Oscar-winning actor or actress (unless that is your dream)! No, what I am begging you to do is answer these questions: What are you doing with your life? What are you becoming as a result of the sweat equity that you invest in your job every single day? Passion is emotional energy channeled in one direction that moves you towards peace of mind and purpose.

A friend of mine, Auke Hempenius, is a prime example of finding your passion without worrying about how much money you will make. He was born in Friesland, the northern province of the Netherlands. For more than twenty years, he pursued many different areas of interest while he searched for his "one true path." One of his career interests was men's fashion. And so it was only natural that he became the co-owner and creative director of an exclusive men's boutique, Milano's Clothier in Winter Park, Florida.

In the many hours he spent at the store, he often found himself asking, "What is my true mission in life?" His answer arrived soon enough. While pondering this question, one of his customers stopped by the boutique and commented that Auke had so much more to offer the world! And the customer asked him, "When are you going to create your own line of clothing?"

At age forty-one, Auke took off to Siesta and Lido Keys near Sarasota, Florida, for four days, to walk the beach, contemplate his future, and prepare to turn his vision into reality. He decided to create his own brand of fine men's clothing, to include a collection of entirely handmade, limited edition suits priced from $1,500 to $6,000, shirts at $295, ties from $125 to $495 and shoes at $895. He was committed to making his label an even greater brand than Zegna, Armani or Brioni! In other words, he planned to do for men's fashion what Ritz Carlton did for luxury hotels.

He later informed the customer who had urged him to follow his dream about his quickly developing plans. The customer promptly invested $10,000 in Auke's venture. Auke took the financing and flew to Florence, Italy, to attend Pitti Uomo, a semi-annual tradeshow for the men's wear industry, and Idea Biella, a fabric tradeshow. Along the way, he was introduced to Ralph Anania, the president of the Worldwide Association of Clothing Designers & Manufacturers. Anania was so impressed with Auke's passion for the business and overall vision, that he invited him to speak at the world conference in Naples the next month, and connected him with all of the key contacts throughout Italy that would assist him in bringing his dream to fruition.

As in many cases with people who pursue their passion, as Auke continued to work his dream, more people continued to show up at the right time and the right place to help make it a reality. This is what some would call 'synchronicity' — when everything happens at once. Eventually Auke launched his dream with $500,000 of seed money from investors who believed in his dream. His first big client was Neiman Marcus. Auke retells the story of landing the Neiman's account with vivid clarity: "When I met with the men's fashion director, who controls over $100 million dollars in purchasing power, I arrived wearing a fedora hat, a cashmere overcoat and scarf, a chocolate-brown matching attaché and garment bag, a Solaro suit, and a boutonniere in my lapel."

I asked Auke, "Why go to such lengths for the appointment?" Auke then went on to describe how Derrill Osborne, the legendary former fashion director for Neiman Marcus, wore a similar ensemble as his daily adornment (it was his signature trademark). My friend had obviously done his homework! More importantly, Auke was able to convert his success at Neiman Marcus into even greater momentum for the development of his brand, as he continued to build his relationships with boutique stores across the country.

On July 19, 2003, Auke launched his brand in the Frank Lloyd Wright Suite at the world-renowned Plaza Hotel in New York City. After Neiman Marcus among other top men's retailers decided they had more pressing priorities than attending the historic global launch of Auke's brand at The Plaza in New York, it became clear it was time to regroup. Instead of being devastated and at wit's end Auke knew that every cloud has a silver lining. Negotiations started to give Auke's brand its own home to showcase the complete collection. After more than a year later with feature articles in The Robb Report and Florida Trend behind him, Auke acquired the space where four years earlier he created one of the best multibrand men's specialty boutiques in the country. It was the most difficult year of his career by far; the endless financial negotiations taught him patience and added business savvy to his substantial creative talents.

His sartorial journey culminated in the grand opening of Auke of Winter Park. If you travel to the Orlando area, make sure you visit the man who has proven that a purpose derived from the soul is not called work.....it is a calling!

Now you understand how Auke Hempenius earned his Italian nickname "The Dutch Vesuvius."

Actor Jack Palance, in his Oscar-winning portrayal of Curly the trail boss in City Slickers, said the secret to happiness is one thing. The challenge is to find out what that thing is for you. Auke found that "one thing"; now what about you?

Wake up! You've been sleepwalking through life long enough. The answer that you've been looking for is inside of

you! Wake up and smell the coffee-the aroma of fresh opportunity that is all around you. This is the moment that you
have been waiting for all of your life. Wake up and go for it!
"Good morning and welcome to Simon's Bakery, what type of
bagel would you like to have today? Do you want it plain or
with cream cheese?"

Follow these simple *Simon Says* pointers.

Simon Says:

- List the things that make you come alive

- Describe decisions you will have to make in order to
  do more of the things that make you come alive.

- List activities that will improve your quality of life and
  take you out of the rat race.

- Like Nike, just do it! Partake in the activities listed
  above.

- Describe your own bagel moment. Enjoy!

SIMON SAYS....DREAM

SIMON SAYS....DREAM

CHAPTER TWO

Simon Says, "Get a Life"

"Most of us live life like fans at an NFL game. We stand on the edge of the playing field, observing the contenders. We stare and cheer, we boo and hiss, but it never occurs to us that we should be on the field."

-T.D. Jakes

Are you happy? Post September 11, 2001, and war with Iraq, people all over the globe are realizing that their lives are worth more than a paycheck, a title on a business card, and a W-2 tax form at the end of the year. In life we must resolve the internal struggle of passion versus paycheck! There are so many "should've, could've, would've" personalities that have passed through our lives over the years. At some level they have left the residue of limited thinking on our hearts. When are you going to move and start LIVING your life? Let this thought soak in for a moment: How many people do you know who walk around making EXCUSES for remaining tenured in a "stuck" position that lacks opportunity?

A Petition for Passion

Are you excited about your life? If you never received a dime of compensation for your daily labor, would you do it anyway? Why are these questions significant? The payment is in what you are **BECOMING** instead of what you are doing. The doing is the transactional part of life; becoming has every-thing to do with what is happening in your being. In other words, we are accustomed to investing forty hours of energy per week in exchange for a paycheck. How many hours per week, however, do we invest in working our passion? What do we get in exchange for working at our passion?

If we make the decision to funnel energy into our areas of passion, the payoff is the discovery of why we were born; the understanding of our individual purpose or purposes on Earth; and finally determining our own net worth. That is the cradle of passion! Fulfillment is the natural payment for living a life of passion. Did you know that the best hand that will feed you is the one at the end of your wrist? Passion is the action! Passion is your "field of dreams." Passion is magical. Passion asks why instead of how. Passion is the oil that keeps your dream engine moving. Passion has an unlimited bank account and writes a cashier's check to pay off the debt of mediocrity. *Sound good so far? Let's further examine this essential element of life...*

Passion doesn't look for a handout only a hand up. Passion rescues you from the ocean of self-limiting beliefs. Passion throws you a life preserver and pulls you toward your shore of opportunity. Passion is the seasoning salt of life. Passion ushers you to the altar of destiny. Passion provides moisture for a dry tear duct. Passion keeps the heart beating when the enemy....*en-a-me* (the enemy inside of you and me that prevents us from being full of passion) wants to pull the plug. A living example of overcoming obstacles and working your passion is Marion Bremshe. Read her story, and be inspired.

In 1982, Marion Luna Bremshe was a full-time mother, a college student and a part-time switchboard operator at a Dallas, Texas, car dealership. During the same year, Marion sought treatment for a lump in her left breast. By 1984, she battled cervical and breast cancer, and wore a wig to hide the side effects of chemotherapy. She was given only five years to live, and was facing $500,000 in hospital bills that insurance wouldn't cover. Her marriage collapsed during this time, and Marion was left to rear two sons, ages fourteen and eight. With little experience, she had to look for additional work in the male-dominated field of auto sales. She applied for a job at sixteen auto dealerships and was turned down at each of them! She went to the seventeenth dealership and the general manager said, "I've been thinking about hiring a broad, lately. And you seem like the nervy type." In spite of this less-than-enlightened management, Marion seized her opportunity in sales. She had a dream of taking control of her life and she pursued this dream with all the zeal she could muster.

In one year she was crowned Salesman of the Year, and given a man's Rolex watch, and tickets to the Super Bowl. Five years later, she owned her own dealership. She found that she had a passion for business ventures. She developed a portfolio that included commercial real estate and a big chunk of a local bank, among other investments.

Her reality of a near-death experience collided with her dreams of entrepreneurship. This collision created the desire, energy and motivation to work passionately towards her dreams. She has been quoted as saying, "Anytime you take a tiny peek at death like I did, you live life with more urgency." She is now happy and in control of her life!

If a woman facing terminal illness and her support system falling apart can find a way to discover her passions and work at them, can't you? Allow your passion to be all that it can be for you . Passion is the wind beneath your wings. It is the unseen force behind every dreamer and doer.

Please do yourself a favor. **"GET A Life!"** Find your passion. Pitch a tent right in the middle of the road and hang a sign that says, "Work in Progress!" Use the following *Simon Says* tips to get started.

Simon Says:

- Determine your passion. Use the vivid examples and definitions in this chapter to help you. Remember, your passion is the one talent or several talents on which you can rely. Passion is the dream or dreams you recurrently have! It's what you do in your spare time or constantly volunteer to do, and you feel wonderful about!

- List activities that you are currently engaged in that you are passionate about.

- On a scale from one to ten, with ten the highest level, rate the level of happiness or joy in your life today.

- Determine ways to maintain or increase your levels of happiness or joy by pursuing your passion.

- Make a list of people or things that hinder, instead of help, in pursuit of your passion.

- Make an action plan of how you will move on past the obstacles in your life.

SIMON SAYS....DREAM

SIMON SAYS....DREAM

CHAPTER THREE

Simon Says, "Live, Work and Play to Your Strengths"

"When we determine what we want and discover ways to get it, we tap into new sources of energy. We uncover a reason to get up every day and have a ball. Sometimes all it takes is asking, what's next in my life?"

- Dave Ellis, author

Nadine Stair, a ninety-three-year old woman in Louisville, Kentucky, had this to say during a recent interview: "If I had my life to live over, I would dare to make more mistakes next time. I would relax. I would limber up. I would be sillier than I've been this time. I would take fewer things seriously, and I would take more chances. I'd take more trips. I'd climb more mountains and I'd swim more rivers. I would eat more ice cream and less beans. I would perhaps have more actual troubles, but I'd have fewer imaginary ones. You see, I am one of those people who lived sensibly and sanely, hour after hour, day after day. Oh, I've had my moments, but if I had it to do over again, I'd have more of them. In fact, I'd try to have nothing else—just moments—one after another instead of living so many years ahead. I've been one of those persons who never goes anywhere without a thermometer, a hot-water bottle, a raincoat, and a parachute. If I had my life to live over, I would start barefoot earlier in the spring, and I would stay that way until the fall. I would go to more dances. I would ride more merry-go-rounds. I would pick more daisies."

When you reach the end of your life, will you be able to say the following?

- I took risks instead of always playing it safe

- I saw the world

- I laughed more instead of being so serious

How old are you? Forgive me for asking, but if you are younger than ninety-three years of age, like myself, then you have no excuse for not living life to its fullest! To live life to its fullest, we must operate from a position of strength by using what we have. There are three steps to tapping into strengths. Are you ready to pursue your heart's desire? If so, buckle up. Here we go...

Strengthen your Strength!

What is one thing that you do better than anyone else you know? What is your core strength? What gives you the greatest enjoyment and satisfaction? Did you know that your strength is really the release of the playful side of your being? One of the common questions people ask is, "How do you recognize your strengths or passion which may not be self-apparent?" In April of 1976, nineteen-year-old, Patricia Cornwell met Ruth Graham, wife of Billy Graham, in Montreat, North Carolina. The Grahams lived down the street. Patricia had the privilege of writing the first version of Mrs. Graham's biography when she was a 24-year-old police reporter who by then had immersed herself into the homicide division. Mrs. Graham gave her just the spark she needed when she gave Patricia her first leather-bound journal and told her she should be a writer. This inspired her to create her first fictional character, forensic pathologist Dr. Kay Scarpetta, who wants to leave the world a little better than she found it. Patricia was amazed that Mrs. Graham would even notice her, let alone take the time to encourage her to pursue writing. Patricia said "Why else would she notice that I played baseball and tennis better than the boys, or wrote poetry and songs and was lonely?" The thriller writer's career was sparked at a neighbor's house.

Who is close to you that really knows you? Ask these people to tell you what they see in you. What are those natural talents or abilities they see in you that you cannot see yourself? They may just share with you the most incredible insight about your personality, gifts or characteristics that make you special. Once you receive feedback from them, then decide if you agree or disagree and what you are going to do to pursue it.

I believe your wealth is hidden in your passion. What is my definition of wealth? It is knowing who you are, what skills, abilities, talents, gifts you possess, and knowing how to leverage them to create a meaningful life. This is what I call spiritual wealth. When you discover your strength and exercise it on a regular basis, then you begin attracting situations, opportunities and people who will show up in your life as if they've been summoned to help you on the path to your desirable future. How does this happen? It is the result, of you tapping into your treasure chest of spiritual wealth. I discovered my spiritual wealth in December 2000, while in Paris giving a presentation to 1,000 leaders from Barclays Bank of London. That day, I stepped through a major doorway of believing in my ability to make a difference. I realized I had something special, and if I didn't recognize it and leverage it, then I would forever live with regret. The feedback that I received from my colleagues and audience participants that day was astounding, and many were impacted while I was talking. One woman told me that she had goose bumps during my speech and it was not due to air conditioning. Another woman said that there was a burning sensation that she felt during my delivery. After hearing this a few times in Paris I came alive to the fact that I had something to offer the world, and if I didn't passionately pursue this gift of speaking I would be a dream pauper.

I found my voice in Paris. I found my unique ability. For the first time I realized that I didn't have to sound like anyone else, be like anyone else, mimic anyone else. I stepped on that stage and saw an ocean of 1,000 souls in front of me, and as I began to talk, each sentence became effortless and my confidence level began to rise. In Paris I discovered "the me" I had always wanted to be. I embraced the wealth in my spirit, which came as a result of me doing what I was most passionate about. It was my turning point in my life when I knew that I had to pursue this gift of speaking so that I could inspire 10 percent of the seven billion people on the planet to find their passion, like me, and live up to their full potential.

Doing what you do best is working your passion. Be passionate about your time, talent and resources. At this juncture you will discover the true meaning for living and loving. When you tap into the well of your greatest potential, it will seem as if time just escapes you because your heart is captured by passion, which releases your spiritual wealth.

Invest in your Strength!

Did you know that some people spend more money on what they put on their heads than what they put in their heads? Did you know that some people use their video rental membership cards more than they use their library cards? When was the last time you attended a professional development workshop? Did you learn anything useful? What are you doing differently as a result of it?

Once you uncover what you are good at, then it is your responsibility to invest in yourself. Buy every book, tape, compact disc, and attend every course that enables you to obtain a firsthand understanding of your area of expertise.

Donald Watkins is a fifty-three-year-old man who lives on the South side of Birmingham, Alabama. He drives to work in a black Chevrolet Impala. Twenty-five years ago he began investing in the financial markets. This was something that he had strong interest in, so he prepared himself by reading and studying how money works. Today, his net worth is estimated at $1.5 billion, and he is considered to be the richest person in Alabama. In his book *The Alchemist*, Paulo Coelho says, "Having a hunch is really intuition, then suddenly there is an immersion of the soul into the universal current of life, where the histories of all people are connected, and we are able to know everything because it's all written there." The more you become comfortable with who you are and invest in yourself, the more your spirit will be open to unlimited possibilities and new realities, which can come by way of hunches or thoughts, even a soft whisper in the center of your being.

I would say Coelho's definition of a hunch was certainly true for Donald Watkins, who followed his hunch with passion and preparation. Today, Watkins owns three jets, a bank, and most recently, was negotiating to purchase 100 percent ownership in the Minnesota Twins, which would make him the first African-American to own a major league baseball team! All of this began when he saved $2,000 back in the 1960s by working in his grandfather's plumbing company in Clarksville, Tennessee. He passionately read every book on investing, invested as a result of his diligence, and now is traveling in the same circles as, say, New York Yankees owner, George Steinbrenner. Coelho says, and I adamantly agree, "When you want something, the entire universe conspires to help you achieve it."

Play to your Strength!

Once you discover your passion and special ability, then it is time to transform your work into play. What would it be like to work hard but to play harder? When you play, it doesn't matter how much you get paid, because the real payment is the exhilarating feeling of satisfaction that you receive when you do what you love. If you check my personal journal, you will find under July 9, 2000:

> I want to communicate the words of life to the nations of the world for the rest of my life. I am willing to work hard on my own craft. If it means rising every single day at 4:00 A.M. to dedicate three hours of my life's energy to my passion, then I am willing to do it.

Playing to your strength is really about entering a state of flow, or as I like to say, "a place of synchronicity when everything happens at once." Imagine entering into a spiritual state where you slow down in order to move faster, sharper and with more precise clarity of purpose! Playing to your strength has everything to do with finding a place of quietness where you begin to create pictures on the movie screen of your imagination.

Playing to your strength means that you live life by divine purpose instead of playing an extra in another person's movie. What do you enjoy doing? What is the one thing you used to dream about when you were a child? Are you living out this dream or are you living out someone else's script for your life? Today is the opportune time for you to get a life and play with a purpose! One of the key ideas for learning how to play to your strength is to examine your current job or business. Are you using gifts or abilities on a daily basis or are you just making money just to be making money?

I remember moving to Research Triangle Park, North Carolina, in 1990 to take a job making more money. These were the early days when Research Triangle Park was just starting to take off and people were moving there on a daily basis. I decided to join the crowd and take the offer because I needed a changed of scenery. The entire time I was in North Carolina I felt out of place. I was not leveraging my strength. I had a great job, nice boss and tons of weekend activities in Chapel Hill to keep me busy. But there was something missing and I couldn't put my finger on it. The only way to describe it was that I was out of sync. I was not playing to my strength. If anything, I was going through the motions. I was spiritually impoverished and just existing.

One day I called Julie Johnson, a friend who lived in Atlanta, Georgia. As I was sharing my frustration with life, work and loneliness she told me about a job opportunity back in Atlanta and it sounded as if it was tailor-made for me. I interviewed over the phone for the job, accepted it immediately, despite a significant reduction in salary, resigned from my job, negotiated my way out of my apartment lease and relocation expenses, packed up my 1986 black Volkswagen Jetta and drove back to Atlanta. While driving down the interstate highway, I begin to reflect on my three-month experience of living in North Carolina and was wondering why I made the move. That day I realized that if you always do something for money then you are never guaranteed true happiness. If you do something because you love it, however, then the payment is the spiritual exhilaration you feel when your heart skips a beat because of authentic happiness. I moved back to Atlanta and started playing to my strengths and within one year I was selected Manager of the Year at my company and received an unexpected financial reward for this honor. Did I take this job for the money? Of course not! I took a cut in pay because the job would allow me to play. As a result, in the end I gained a far greater reward, and I learned a valuable lesson that has shaped my life even today.

These simple *Simon Says* will help you get to this point in your life.

Simon Says:

- Make a list of your strengths. Use the tips and examples within this chapter to help you discover them!

- With your new, expanded definition of wealth, assess your own wealth.

- Determine what areas of your life you can further develop to increase your wealth.

- Determine what ways you can invest in your strength.

- List ways that you can play to your strength.

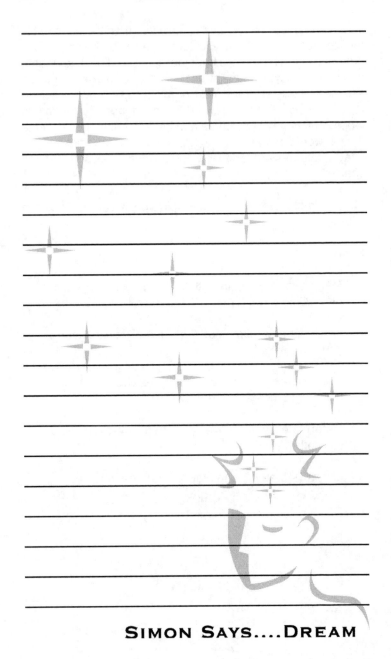

SIMON SAYS....DREAM

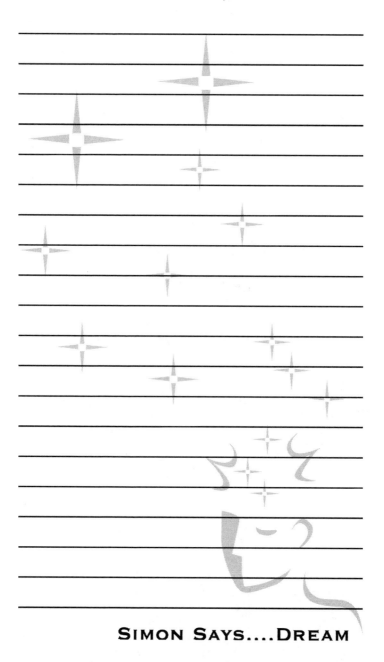

SIMON SAYS....DREAM

CHAPTER FOUR

Simon Says,
"What You See Is What You Get"

"You know the story of the three brick masons. When the first man was asked what he was building, he answered gruffly, without even raising his eyes from his work, 'I'm laying bricks.' The second man replied, 'I'm building a wall.' But the third man said enthusiastically and with obvious pride, 'I'm building a cathedral.'"

-Margaret Stevens

If you can see the invisible, then you can do the impossible! This morning I spent some quality time meditating about the upcoming day, and then all of sudden, images of incredible possibilities began to develop within my mind. I began to see pictures of my future, and how living my dream and being first class was a possible reality, instead of being far away in a distant galaxy. When was the last time you planned a vacation? Do you recall doing all of the research by calling a travel agent, researching the potential location via the Internet, or even asking friends about a popular destination? It's amazing to me that sometimes we plan our personal and family vacations better than we plan our lives! Our vacations are usually two weeks in length, but we live sixty to eighty years on Earth! Do we spend as much time planning for sixty to eighty years of living as we do for two weeks vacation? Probably not!

Dave Hegan, a successful steel-processing mogul tells a similar story. In the late 1980s, Hegan was, by his own account, "a spectacularly unsuccessful burglar-alarm salesman" consistently ranking dead last in weekly sales. During a 1988 golf game, Hegan told a partner precisely how he planned to get on the eighteenth green: "Hit the ball 200 yards, curve it forty yards from left to right, and drop it six feet from the hole." He did exactly that! Astonished, his colleague demanded to know his secret. Hegan said, "I practiced for years. I trained. I had in my mind's eye what I was trying to do. And that's when it hit me," Hegan recalls, "That's how the great salesmen do it. They practice. They train. I realized that if I worked as hard at selling as I did at golf, I'd never look back." Hegan left the course and started two years of self-directed sales training. He read books, listened to tapes and attended seminars. Within two months, Hegan was heading his group in sales. Today, Hegan is president of Majac Steel, a steel-processing company in East Chicago, Indiana. The company's revenues have grown by 878 percent since 1996!

Let's discuss the method that I use to create a positive picture of unlimited opportunities within my mind's eye. However,
we need to answer a few questions that will provide a context
to our discussion as you discover these principles. What is
your dream? What is your vision of the future? What images
are flashing on the movie screen of your mind? The picture
that stays in your mind will happen in time. What you continue to focus on will eventually end up the feature film of your
life. Do you want what you see or do you see what you want?
Program the movie reel of your life with pictures of coming
attractions starring you! Run the preview picture you want to
see—the future you! Know that seeing is believing!

Barbara Corcoran, was the second of ten children and was
reared in Edgewater, New Jersey. Her father was a printing
press manager. Her stay-at-home mom was the general who
ran their small army of a family. At age seven, Corcoran
struggled to read. Teachers put her in a class for students
with learning disabilities. "Don't worry about it," her mother
said. "You have a wonderful imagination, Barbara Ann."
Throughout her life she had twenty-six jobs but always
believed that there was more for her to do. She said in her
new autobiography about her life, "I had one image of myself
and one goal. I saw myself as the queen of New York real
estate."

Prior to finding her path, however, she had to live through the
stinging pain of the words from her first business partner who
told her, "You'll never succeed without me." It was this same
business partner that she had fallen in love with and moved
in with to help raise his children. But the romance ended
badly. He fell in love with one of the assistants that worked in
Barbara's company. He decided to marry the assistant and
because he controlled the majority of the firm, refused to let
Corcoran fire the woman. For two years, Barbara lived with
the situation, ashamed to confront him. She said, "He left me.
And I wasn't confident enough that I didn't deserve it." She
eventually did confront him and resolved the situation, and

then refocused on the picture she saw in her mind's eye. Today, some 20 years later, at age 52, she chairs the Corcoran Group, a 500-agent residential brokerage firm in New York City. This amazing outcome was from someone who mentally created a picture and pursued her dream despite the obstacles.

Did you know that the images in our minds anchor us to our past, our present and our future? Where have you dropped your mental anchors? Some people have chosen to keep their ship of future possibilities anchored at Port Maybe. Are you familiar with this port? It is a port of call that thousands of ships have made into a permanent shipyard. Maybe, instead, you've dropped your anchor in Dream Lake or Hope Bay. These are the destinations from which you can sail to a rewarding future.

Do you remember the movie scene from *Coming to America* when Eddie Murphy and Arsenio Hall are looking at a map of the world and Eddie says he will leave the prosperous land of Zamunda (Africa) and travel to America to find his queen? He spins the globe, and when it stops spinning, his finger points to Queens, New York. When they arrive at the airport, there are three taxicabs that are loaded with Louis Vitton luggage. Do you recall this movie as I describe it? Did you automatically replay this scene in your mind? I transferred a picture to your mind through the power of words. I tapped into your mind's computer system, opened the file folder called movies, and it located the two actors by name, by movie title and by the specific movie scene.

Every single day, images that create emotions, feelings and outcomes are transferred to your mental picture screen by television, by newspaper and by your work environment. Now, imagine if you stop the flashing images by changing the channel. Ladies and gentlemen, the imagination is just that powerful! The key question that we must ask ourselves is, are we leveraging our imaginations to create the future? In this film, Eddie's character, developed tangible (although far-fetched) objectives and executed his plan. What if you did the same thing?

Dream Big

Dr. Dan Bagley who coaches executives in Fortune 500 companies was asked why people don't go for their dreams? He said the following: "People have a fear of failure, and in order to protect themselves from disappointment, they sacrifice their dreams on the altar of complacent safety." Do you know anyone that can relate to this? I sure do. I call them dream squashers. They have put their dreams on lay-a-way and never paid off the balance. Meanwhile, they don't want you to live your dreams either because they believe you'll start thinking that you are better than they are! I have just two words for you: "Dream Big." The bigger you dream the more you will stretch and refuse to return to a comfort zone of small living. You can do it! Go for it! Reach for it!

Here are five dream arrows for you to add to your quiver as you target living a life of purpose:

- Stop living someone else's script.

- March to the beat of your own drum. Be yourself. You are a whole person with a great mind.

- Like Nike, just do it and stop making excuses. Obstacles are what you see when you take your eye off the goal.

- Design your ideal life. Describe it in detail and determine that you are unstoppable.

- Share your dream with others, but be discerning. Identify those who will assist you in making your dream a reality. Invest time, energy and finances in them.

90 Percent of Communication Is Non-verbal

Mike Murdock, a spiritual leader and motivational speaker in Dallas, Texas, says, "Losers look at what they are going through while champions look at what they are going to." Where are you going? Where will you be one year, five years and ten years from now? These are key questions that you must ask yourself. Why? In just a few short years, you are going to wake up and say where did the time go? What did I do with my life?

You are bright, intelligent, sharp, witty and destined to positively impact thousands of lives. I believe this about you. Well, by now you are saying, "Simon how can you say that when you don't even know me?" But the creator of the universe knows you. I sense in my spirit that this is your internal spring season, and you are moving into a new reality of complete clarity. It is spring; let the budding and growth season flourish in your life. Embrace it. Spring is here! It doesn't matter what happened last winter. I am inviting you to let it go. Your days of hibernation and sitting behind the scenes, waiting for your name to be called, are over. Stand up. It's time to come forth because destiny awaits you. Hear this in the deep place of your spirit...the best is yet to come! Do you believe it? Do you see it? I do.

Use these keys to unlocking your imagination. Like any skill, using your imagination effectively takes practice. Try these ideas regularly to stretch your imagination's muscles.

Simon Says:

- **Calm Yourself.** This may be the single most important key to unlocking your imagination. You must trust yourself enough to remove yourself from everyone and everything else to find a quiet place to engage yourself.

- **Close Your Eyes.** As you become more accustomed to tapping into your imaginative energy, closing your eyes will be just as mandatory. Closing one's eyes indicates removal from the limitations of current circumstances, and unlocks the power to think the unthinkable.

- **Listen and Watch.** Building one's imaginative energy can begin by taking everyday words—for example, pencil, flower or running-and successfully transfer an image of these words to your mind's eye. Thinking of these words must produce the idea or concept that you see when your eyes are closed. Practice saying a word, then visualizing the concept.

- **Manifest.** Did you know that our imaginations not only have visual components, but every other sense we possess? You can train your mind with the abilities to "hear" the thoughts of your mind. Your imagination is the vehicle to get you where your heart is already encouraging you to go. You must fuel it with positive, clear images, loaded with sensory information, and allow it to manifest itself through your diligent work.

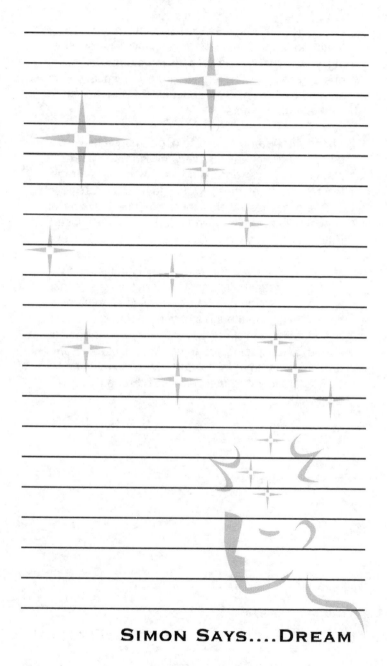

SIMON SAYS....DREAM

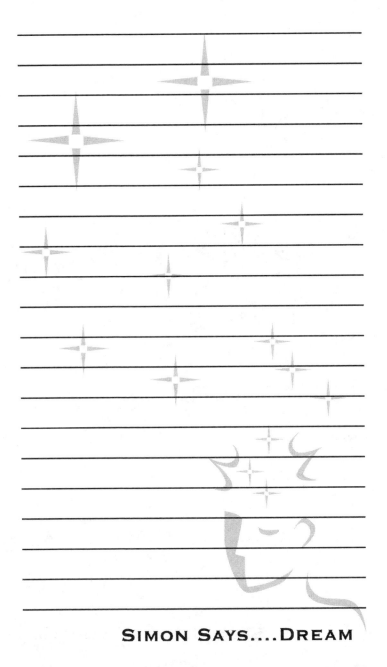

SIMON SAYS....DREAM

CHAPTER FIVE

Simon Says, "Change Lanes"

"Create your own life. Don't let others define you. Remember, you are the driver. Stay in the driver's seat so you can stop, back up, accelerate, or turn. Keep your independence of thought. Enjoy your imagination and dreams."

- Steve Robbins

While driving down an interstate highway recently, I noticed a sign that said: "Slow traffic stay to the right." I said to myself, "Wow that is really interesting." I wonder how many people go through life staying in the right lane all of their lives, while transporting passengers—broken dreams, negative thoughts and emotions, bad habits–that prevent them from accelerating into the future. At this season, my friend, I am inviting you to get off at the next exit. Invite those passengers, who are really the thieves of your time and productivity, to get out of your car and to find a ride elsewhere! Nothing will change until you change lanes and leave the right lane! At Microsoft, Bill Gates admits, "In three years, every product we make is obsolete. The only question is whether we will make them obsolete or someone else will."

Here are three keys to start your engine, accelerate into the future and to embrace change:

Clarity of Purpose

Where are you going? Do you have plan? When was the last time you reviewed the map of your future? When you are clear about who you are, then you understand your purpose and make the most of your life. If you are not clear about your purpose and you don't know what you want to be, what you want to do, or what you want to have, then any road you travel will take you in any direction. In other words, any road will take you to nowhere in particular, which is your unfocused, unplanned destination.

When you know who you are, no matter what happens in life, no matter what setbacks you may experience or even disappointments, you can be steadfast and be assured that everything is going to work out for you, because you are grounded by knowing who you are, what you have and what you can do. There is a purpose for everything and a destination for everyone! Every invention that was ever created has a purpose. Consider a car, a train or an airplane. Although each is a mode of transportation, each has a specific purpose. You must know your destination and purpose for travel to determine which transportation mode will work best for you. Otherwise, you will make choices such as driving a car with only two good tires and a smoking exhaust to work because you did not know a commuter train could get you there faster and more pleasurably!

What are the ways that you can discover your purpose? First, what excites you? What are your hobbies? What gives you complete satisfaction when you are engaged and excited? If you could create the perfect life for yourself what would it be? Where would you live? What would you be doing? The answer to finding your purpose will come only as a result of the quality of your questions. I believe that the quality of your questions will determine the quality of your answers. The quality of your thinking will determine the quality of your life. Now is the appointed time for you to stop wandering aimlessly through life and being afraid to move past GO. Thousands of organizations and companies are downsizing. Many people don't know what they are going to do. They are almost in denial of being laid off. Even people who possess advanced degrees, a Rolodex of contacts and a database of clients have discovered that their entire identity was connected to one company.

When are you going to realize that you are the president of You, Inc.? At You, Inc., you are president and owner of all of your greatest assets: your thoughts, your knowledge, your skills, your talents, your vision, your contacts, and your time! If you are not familiar with You, Inc., why would you be interested in changing lanes? Without this knowledge, you will weave from lane to lane, relationship to relationship, job to job, city to city; never living your passion or vision and maximizing your potential.

Do you really know who you are? Until you discover who you really are, at the core of your being, and what value you bring to the marketplace, companies will only pay you what they think you are worth. When you know how much you are worth, your mind will go to work. You will start creating opportunities for yourself, instead of waiting for someone else to discover you. From November 7, 2001, my personal journal reads:

> I am thirty-three years old and I have been waiting for someone to discover me. I just discovered myself, and I feel good about me.

Map Out the Future

With just a few clicks of a mouse button on your home computer, you can print out driving directions from your house to anywhere in the country! Selecting the key word *travel* on the Internet will enable you to determine the total travel time of the trip, the total distance in miles, and what turnpike or interstate to merge onto from your house to go anywhere in the United States! There is even a route overview map with a zoom-in and zoom-out feature that allows you to visualize your journey from Point A to Point B! The best part, however, is that you can print this map in color. Wow! By now you can almost guess that a metaphor is coming, right? Right!

Plan your life's route! Some people implement this credo, while others, as simple as it seems, start, but never finish. Others start and stop every December or January. Today, make a decision that you will create the best plan possible for your life, and be open to merging, purging and changing lanes at any given moment. Why? It's just a fact of life. Stuff happens. People change. You may experience a business slowdown, company promotions may be backed up , or your 401k retirement plan may head the wrong way. Plan to learn as much as you can, as fast as you can. When you think that you've learned it all, then learn some more!

Transform Your Driving Experience

My dad was my first driving instructor. As a result of his lessons he taught me, and the experience and knowledge that he shared with me, I can now drive in the most challenging conditions. I learned to drive in the parking lot of our neighborhood supermarket after it closed in the evenings. My dad would always say, "Remember that you are driving for the person in front of you, behind, and on both sides of you." He would say with special emphasis, "Simon, whatever you do, keep both hands on the steering wheel at all times!" I remember driving in the snow capitol of the world - Buffalo, New York - my home town, and one of the historic sites for the Underground Railroad. I could hear my dad's voice in my head, "Tap the break lightly to stop in the snow!"

You are more than able to drive through the blizzard of choices and decisions that you will need to make throughout your life. Be encouraged that you are equipped and emotionally intelligent enough to make the best possible decisions because you are brilliant.

Take your left hand and steer your life in the direction of blissful living. Take your right hand and adjust the rearview mirror of yesterday. Remember that you cannot change where you have been, but you can change where you are going. Mike Murdock, spiritual leader and motivational speaker from Dallas, Texas, said, "You can't drive forward looking in a rearview mirror." Broken dreams, forgotten promises, negative thoughts, and small thinking, which may be riding in your backseat, can easily be ejected with just one button.

I have always been fascinated by the James Bond automobiles, equipped with state-of-the-art technology, that allow him to escape near death in the movies. If you have ever seen any of the 007 series, then you know he has a secret eject button and an ejection seat equipped with a parachute, which enables him to stay out of harm's way. Well, I want you

to do the reverse of what 007 does! Today, instead of eject-
ing yourself, I want you to eject those negative, emotionally
draining, pessimistic back seat drivers that are directing your
inner world and inhibiting your view of the possibilities. Today
is the greatest day of your life. The best is yet to come. I
believe it! I know it! I can feel it! Change lanes because your
future depends on it!

Use these *Simons Says* to switch gears into your future:

- List dead-weight issues or people who weigh you
  down in the slower, "Do Not Pass," right lane of life.

- Write an action list detailing how to lighten your load
  of dead-weight obstacles.

- Reference your journal notes from Chapter One;
  note how reconciling purpose is directly linked to
  your passion.

- Describe your own business, You, Inc. What does it
  look like? What are its main products, services and
  key assets?

- Conduct a valuation of You, Inc. What price tag
  would you put on the business? What price would
  you give the value of your contributions?

- Write a plan for fulfilling your purpose or purposes in
  life. Include start dates and end dates, where applic-
  able.

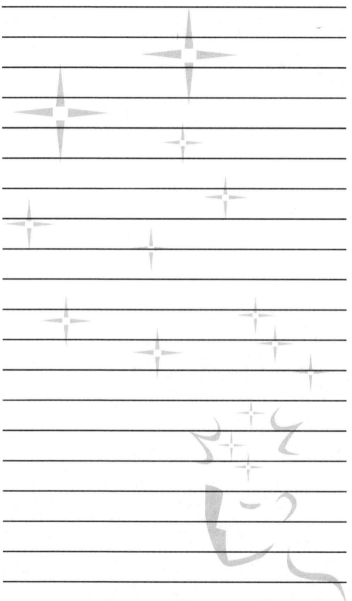

SIMON SAYS....DREAM

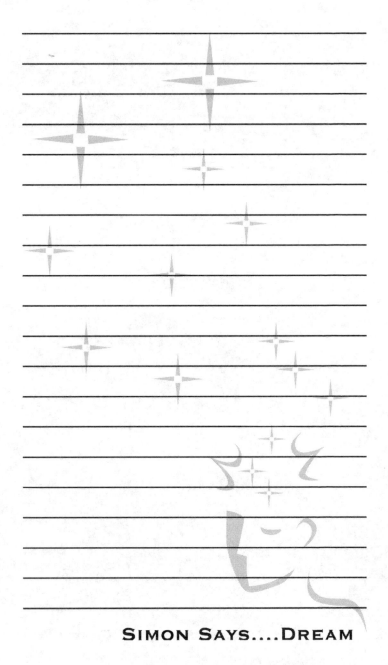

SIMON SAYS....DREAM

CHAPTER SIX

Simon Says,
"Greatness Is Written All over You!"

"To every person there comes that special moment when he is tapped on the shoulder to do a very special thing unique to him. What a tragedy if that moment finds him unprepared for the work that would be his finest hour."

-Winston Churchill

You are destined for greatness! Today you will embark on a journey of discovering who you were created to be and what purpose you were destined to fulfill since the beginning of time.

You are brilliant! I believe there is incredible potential that is hibernating in the depths of your being. I want to evoke in you a hunger and a thirst to move toward action and become the architect of your tomorrow.

A new man-made fountain directly across the Mississippi River from the Gateway Arch in St. Louis, Missouri, is now the world's highest geyser, reaching nearly 630 feet. The Gateway Geyser is powered by three 800-horsepower pumps and discharges water at up to 250 feet per second. It will keep 1,100 gallons of water, weighing 9,200 pounds, in the air when in operation, according to the Gateway Center. I believe, however, the highest and most powerful geyser is in you! Remove the lid sealing your soul's geyser, and witness how high your reach will be!

You were born to soar! This is your year to leap into the future that is desperately waiting for you to wake up and to take your place in the circle of life! Diligently cultivate the greatness within you. I believe that you will experience a metamorphosis in your thinking. What is greatness? It is the ability to experience unspeakable joy in fulfilling your life's purpose. What is freedom? It is the endless volume of air you breathe as you embrace life and realize your full value. Greatness is waiting for you at the intersection of Freedom Lane and Destiny Boulevard!

As you move in the direction of your heart's desire and refrain from comparing your accomplishments to your best friend, co-worker, or college roommate, you will discover it's all good!

There was a time in my life when I contemplated suicide. I

felt as if all of my friends were always receiving the breaks, promotions and all of life's good fortune. Then, there was me, Simon T. Bailey, always a day late and dollar short. Finally, one day I gathered enough nerve and looked in the mirror and said, "Simon you need to LET IT GO." The Comparison Inferiority Complex, or CIC, and the disease called "issue-itis" filled my spirit.

CIC is the acronym I penned to describe the lower-than-low feeling we get when we focus on someone else's journey and accomplishments, opposed to our own. CIC is the disease and "limited thinking" is the awful side effect. It is the disease that festers and makes any issue, no matter how small, inflamed and blown out of proportion I became a man full of issues: relationship issues, work-related issues, money issues and self-esteem issues!

Dr. Mark Chironna, pastor of The Master's Touch International Church, Orlando, Florida, and my life coach advocates: "In the pursuit of your life's purpose, there will strategically occur a defining moment in the form of a refining crisis, setting you free from a confining limitation, thus empowering you to step into greatness!" Suffering from Comparison Inferiority Complex, limited thinking and issue-itis represented the refining crisis for me. How about you? Have you been victim to CIC? Or do you suffer from some other self-limiting, idea-drowning issue? Please allow this chapter and Dr. Chironna's words to inspire you and inform you that these limiting situations can springboard you to greatness. But you do have to work through them.

My life coach diagnosed my key issue with two words: jealousy and comparison. He looked me in the eye and said, "Stop trying to be like everyone else and just be you." When I decided to be myself and to LOVE ME, is when greatness stood up inside of me and said, "What took you so long?" It is sad when people never discover that they were born for greatness, and they carry their potential, creativity and gifts to the grave.

Today, I am free. I cancelled my membership in Issue-itis Anonymous. Dr. Chironna said, "Most people's lives are spent trying to fit in, and all of us need to reach a place in our lives where we leave behind performance-driven relationships." Ridding myself of my friends' old issues was my attempt to release the need to fit in and to shed the necessity to psychoanalyze my friends. Those individuals who could not deal with my new attitude are no longer in my life, and I feel so free! I am a whole person, and it feels so good to live my own script. WOW! There is an awesome feeling being free of the stronghold of yesterday! Let us not forget the familiar saying by George Eliot: "It is never too late to be what you might have been!" Need more convincing? Consider this: In *The Path*, Laurie Beth Jones tells an incredible story about gravitational pull. Apparently most of the fuel that is used by spaceships traveling to the moon is consumed in just getting them beyond Earth's gravity. After a spaceship has done so, NASA scientists count on lunar gravity to pull it toward the moon. According to Jones, "escape velocity" requires the most energy "moving us away from our former way of life." A compelling vision also must be so clear and so powerful that its very magnetism and gravitational forces will literally pull you toward it!

Recognize the greatness in you! Allow these *Simon Says* directions to assist you:

- Define your greatness.

- List any obstacles blocking you from your greatest life experiences.

- Brainstorm ways to remove any obstacles.

- Write your action plan to continue to recognize the greatness within you!

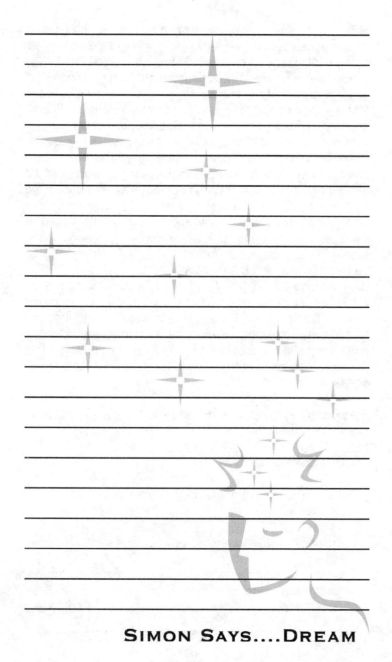

SIMON SAYS....DREAM

SIMON SAYS....DREAM

CHAPTER SEVEN

Simon Says,
"Diamonds Are a Man's Best Friends!"

"Through enthusiastically living a dream defined, we have come to realize that a dream is not an it, it is an us, our spiritual signature, a life-force that is greater than ourselves that works itself through us, awakening the soul, rhythming the heart, and allowing for the changing and growing self."

-Stuart Avery Gold

The richest place in the entire universe is the cemetery. Everyday, there are countless people who take their potential to the grave, never discovering the grand destiny that was available to them. At this season of your journey, I want to invite you to find the diamonds that are located deep in the mine of your soul.

You are priceless! There is so much wealth that exists inside of you that it is impossible for you to measure your net worth, soul worth, and spirit worth! In the late 1800s Russell Conwell wrote *Acres of Diamonds*. In this thought-provoking book, he described a farmer named Ali who heard diamonds were discovered in a land far away. Just the thought of diamonds excited Ali to the point that he sold his farm and equipment to move to this land of tremendous promise.

Ali searched for diamonds from sunrise to sunset. He spent all of his time, energy and life savings searching for the priceless diamonds. He never spent time establishing meaningful relationships because the only thing that mattered was finding diamonds, which he thought were key to his happiness. He believed that once he found those precious jewels, his life would be picture perfect. In fact, he believed that he would buy a ranch nestled between two rolling hills; find a wife, and give her a real diamond instead of a "diamonique." Well, as the story goes, he died and never found the diamonds that he was looking for.

The man to whom Ali sold his farm began surveying his property, and noticed a shiny crystal-like rock partially sticking out of the dirt. He asked one of his farm hands to bring him a shovel. When he began digging into the rich dark soil, he started scooping up diamonds and more diamonds! He shouted to his wife, "Honey, I've found acres of diamonds!"

You are probably saying by now, "Simon what's your point in sharing this story?" The bottom-line is that everything that you need to succeed in life is right underneath your nose. Ali went to find the diamonds somewhere else instead of in his own backyard. Subsequently he went to the grave without ever realizing the great wealth he had actually possessed. Do you know anyone who fits this description?

On several occasions during my personal journey, I tried to mine for diamonds by copying what I saw others doing instead of being true to my values and belief-system. As long as I tried to duplicate the results of others, I denied myself the discovery of riches from my own diamond mine. I didn't believe in the wealth of my potential. As a man, I was intimidated by anybody who was doing better, earning more and dressing finer. In *The Enemy Called Average*, author John Mason states it plainly: "People are born originals, but most die copies." That's the direction I was headed!

My low self-esteem caused me to search for love in all the wrong faces, in all the wrong places. Then I read *Acres of Diamonds*, and it changed my life. I discovered the eternal wealth that was lying dormant in the core of my spirit. I began to change my spiritual diet by feasting on the diamond opportunities. As a result, my mind began to change, life began to change, and I began to feel and think better about tomorrow. I found my diamond mine and so can you. Diamonds are waiting to be discovered by you.

Harris Rosen, a 61-year-old hotelier from New York City found himself in 1970 on a path that would lead to Orlando. His entrepreneurial spirit was born in the streets of New York, but his work ethic came from his father, who worked at the posh Waldorf Astoria Hotel as a full-time director of safety and part-time artist. As a result, Rosen was bitten by the hotel bug and decided to attend Cornell University, where he studied the hotel business. He also made his mark in his fraternity, Tau Epsilon Phi, as the one member of the pledge class who refused to be hazed. He went to work for one of the largest entertainment companies in Orlando. After three years, he was convinced that he never wanted to work for anyone else but himself again. He said, "I thought I did a great job, but I never really fit in, according to my supervisors." Rosen went on to build his Orlando hotel empire through long hours, an eye for cost cutting and virtually no debt. In 1974, Rosen bought his first hotel at a time when other hoteliers were looking to get out of the business. There was trouble in the Middle East, including an oil embargo, which was constricting tourism. Rosen grabbed a 256-room Quality Inn hotel on International Drive, in the heart of Orlando' s bustling tourism corridor for $150,000 and an agreement to assume a $2.5 million mortgage.

Rosen moved into the hotel, where he would live for more than seven years. He did the gardening and landscaping; when dinner time came, he carved the roast beef in the hotel's restaurant; he carried guests' luggage to their rooms; and after hours, he and his beloved German shepherd, Rinny, would patrol the grounds. Today, his company has more than 3,500 employees, offers English language classes, a staff doctor and health-care clinic, college tuition for workers and their families and an outreach center where employees are helped with numerous issues, such as finding a mechanic who won't take advantage of a Spanish-speaking worker.

Rosen has also given a couple of million dollars for scholarships to the University of Central Florida, Rosen School of Hospitality Management, which dreams of offering free tuition, allowing the program to pick from the best students in the country. Mr. Rosen is one of the most brilliant men in the hospitality industry today. His mother often told him "I don't care what you do. Just make sure you do it well." Mr. Rosen found his acres of diamonds when he embraced his passion for hospitality.

Try this list of *Simon Says* suggestions to find your diamond mine!

Simon Says:

- Review your list of strengths from Chapter Two.

- Review the activities or opportunities that enable you to exercise those strengths.

- Develop a plan to partake in those activities as much as possible.

- Commit to yourself. Take a solemn vow to implement the plan.

- At least once a day, remember to repeat these affirmations with power, passion and emotion:
  - I am rich!
  - I am priceless!
  - I am valuable!
  - I am living my dream!
  - I am finding my own diamonds!

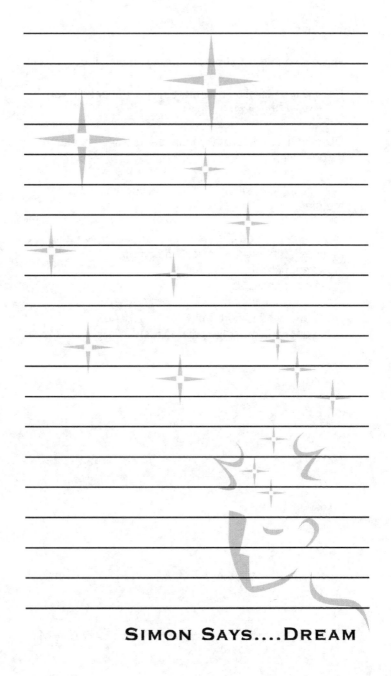

SIMON SAYS....DREAM

SIMON SAYS....DREAM

CHAPTER EIGHT

Simon Says, "Think First Class!"

"It is not our environment, it is you—the quality of your minds, the integrity of your souls, and the determination of your wills—that will decide your future and shape your lives."

-Benjamin E. Mays

Flying coach class on any major airline is really a pain. I am sitting by the window observing the incredible artistic design of an airplane wing and dreaming about sitting in first class. Please understand that my purpose in sharing this story is to awaken the first-class thinking that resides in all us when we decide that it's time for a change. Wow! the view of the sky is incredible, and even though the plane is traveling at 500 to 600 miles per hour, looking outside feels like the plane is not moving at all. The emotional energy of mediocrity in coach class is draining.

Have you ever experienced a "coach-class moment?" You may ask the flight attendant if they are serving any meals on a three-hour flight, and the flight attendant says in a low voice, "No!" But you hold your head up and take a sneak peek through the curtains of the first-class cabin and discover a whole new world. There are only sixteen seats in the first-class cabin, but there are two attendants passing out hot towels, dining place mats, and also taking drink orders. Then, suddenly, you smell food, but you can't see it! You hear the flight attendant asking the first-class passenger, "Is everything all right?" and "Can I get you anything else?"

Meanwhile, your stomach begins to churn with hunger pains because you and your two coach-class neighbors have nothing but a royal feast of peanuts! The flight attendants have memorized the beverage menu and offer you a free beverage. If I want alcohol, it's going to cost me four dollars. As I look into first class I see the flight attendants pouring drinks into a *glass*, and they are not collecting any greenbacks in exchange for a beverage! What do I do? Consistent with my coach-class feeling, I say give me the FREE non-alcoholic beverage. The flight attendant gives me a *plastic cup* and asks me if I want the full can of soda, as if she is doing me a favor!

Can you relate to what I am saying? In life, at one time or another, we have all been stuck in the cheap seats! Today I have discovered a whole new meaning for living: I don't have to sit in first class to be first-class. Sitting in coach doesn't mean that I am confined to coach mentality. If anything, I am an individual who appreciates the finer things in life, but I don't need to sit in First Class to impress you or to make you think that I am somebody special.

The real question that we must ask our heart instead of our head is: what do I have to BECOME in order to be first-class in everything I think, do, say and feel. Now, the prefix for the word become is: be. What is the message in your innermost being?

Today, decide that where you are does not determine what you can be or do or have in life. Invest in relationships that are congruent with your core values. Dare to dream and reach for something bigger, greater and larger than ever before. Morrie Schwartz, who is profiled in *Tuesdays with Morrie*, said this: "Look, no matter where you live, the biggest defect we human beings have is our shortsightedness. We don't see what we could be. We should be looking at our potential, stretching ourselves into everything we can become. But if you're surrounded by people who say 'I want mine now,' you end up with a few people with everything, and a military to keep the poor ones from rising up and stealing it."

When I decided to look within myself, I discovered that my circumstance was nothing more than the circle in which I was standing in. But, I continued to subject myself to playing small, thinking small and living small. This has everything to do with self-worth and how I saw myself.

I remember living in a studio apartment in Atlanta, Georgia, called Peyton Place. This was a drug-infested neighborhood, and the place that I called home. I didn't have a car but smiled every time I got on MARTA (Moving African-Americans Rapidly through Atlanta), the public transportation system. Why did I smile? I knew that one-day I would have a nice brand new shiny car and wouldn't have to depend on the accuracy of a train schedule. In my studio apartment, there were a few possessions that meant so much to me—my bed, which was simply a mattress on the floor, my bright-green bean bag chair from the 1970s, the milk crates, which served as a television stand, my high school ring, and my twenty-five-dollar Bolex (cousin of Rolex), which I purchased in New York City. In my refrigerator was a carton of milk and a can of tuna. I was on the Atkins diet and didn't even know it. Oh, did I mention that I had roommates who would make their uninvited appearance from time to time, but wouldn't stay long? I called them Mr. Roach and Mr. Mouse.

Nevertheless, I began to think my way into a better future. I refused to live in these deplorable conditions. At one point, I said to myself, "If the nuns of St. James Catholic School (Buffalo, New York) could see me now, I could just imagine a paddle making contact with a part of my anatomy where the sun doesn't shine." Something had to change. At the time, I was only making five dollars and ten cents per hour working as a front desk clerk at the Days Inn Downtown Atlanta, which was down the street from the Greyhound Bus Station. As you can imagine, business was booming, but I was not getting ahead.

One day a friend of mine invited me to a monthly meeting of the Hospitality Sales and Marketing Association International that was being held at the JW Marriott Hotel in Buckhead, on the north side of town. I lived on the south side (you get the picture). While attending the meeting in my twenty-dollar, three-button black suit from my favorite consignment shop, I met Ed Staros.

At the time, he was the managing director of the Ritz-Carlton Buckhead, the flagship hotel in the Ritz-Carlton Chain. He gave me his card and told me to call him. As I departed that evening to return to my hood, I said to myself, "What in the world would this white man want with me, the brother from the dark side of town?" I called him a few days later to give the impression that I wasn't needy, but was doing him a favor, and he invited me to meet with him and the hotel manager. I said, "Sure, not a problem, let me just move some appointments and we can meet." Little did he know that the only appointment movement was when I switched my work schedule with another hourly employee.

I met with Mr. Staros and he offered me a job as night manager for the Ritz-Carlton Buckhead, making three times what I was earning at the Days Inn front desk. I told him that I had to think about it. Up until that time, my entire life was built on playing it safe. I thought about it and said to myself, "Why should I go and work on that side of town when there is no one who looks like me. Who do I think I am? I know nothing about passing the Grey Poupon, and it's expensive to live in Buckhead. I will just return to the Days Inn Downtown and tell them I should be put in management. I would leverage the Ritz-Carlton offer to stay in my comfort zone. The year was 1988; I was only twenty years old and clueless in Atlanta. In my mind, I was not good enough to work at the Ritz. My coach-class mentality had once again kept me confined to a limited place. I turned down the job at the Ritz.

Several years later I realized my mistake. It was at this very moment when the feeling of unworthiness and small thinking had to be addressed. I started reading *Think and Grow Rich: A Black Choice* by Dennis Kimbro. This book inspired to me to begin thinking about what was possible instead of what was impossible. It was a wake up call for me to get my act together. It was time to upgrade my thinking by surrounding myself with positive people who really believed in me. I needed to know if a friend was really a friend, or just an acquaintance, because whoever has your ear has your life.

Some people are very comfortable thinking coach class. They are comfortable with the results they are generating.

There is nothing wrong with being happy right where you are; however, there are a few of us who've decided to upgrade how we (passionate people) view life, and we have decided to create the future instead of waiting for the future to happen. We've decided to think for ourselves instead of letting others tell us what to think.

At some level I look back now at the Ritz Carlton opportunity and think that it was one of my biggest mistakes in my life; on the other hand, I realize that I made the best decision I could make at the time and the path I followed has helped me discover who I am.

First-class thinking is available to anyone who wants to be the best; however it is reserved for those who put their feet in motion and move towards destiny!

Consider these questions as you move forward with your life:

- What are you doing to increase your value?

- What have you learned about yourself in the last 12 months?

- What new behaviors have you adapted for your life?

First-class thinking is not for some, it is for everyone! Incorporate these questions as food for thought. Use these *Simon Says* suggestions to motivate you to a bigger, brighter, first-class future

Simon Says:

- List your most vivid "coach-class moments."

- Write your own "first-class thinking" statement.

- Describe activities that you can participate in that will support your first-class thoughts.

- List any ideas or activities that you will have to eliminate because they are inconsistent with your first-class mentality.

SIMON SAYS....DREAM

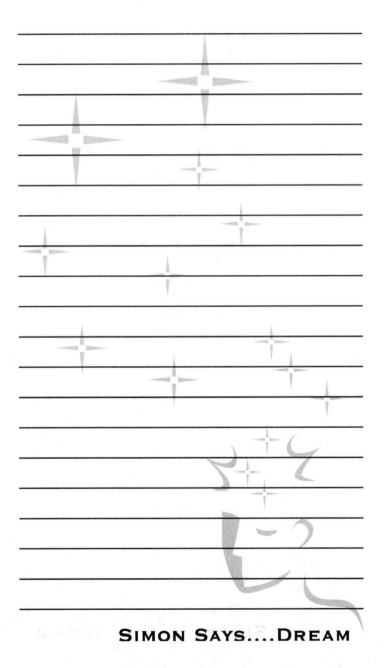

SIMON SAYS....DREAM

CHAPTER NINE

Simon Says,
"Dump the Files and Reboot Your Life"

"When we link our happiness and well-being to jobs, possessions, looks, and money, we become attached to them. We make our roles more important than our souls."

-Dave Ellis

Have you ever worked on a computer project and found your-self going to bed early (before 9:30 P.M.) so that you could wake up promptly at 3:30 A.M.? Have you ever turned on your computer only to find that it was slower than normal? Well, recently I was completing a very important assignment before deadline, and my computer had a mind of its own! I turned it on, and my hourglass icon was frozen on the screen! Then, in my infinite wisdom, I used the control+alter+delete keys—the command to shut the system down. For whatever reason the computer still would not restart. By now, fumes were coming out my nostrils and I was blowing steam like a runaway locomotive! (Rest assured the problems with this PC were not the result of the operator.)

After a couple hours of trying the same thing and getting the same result, I called a friend, who is a computer wizard, to solicit help in rescuing my sick PC. He asked several direct questions, and we discovered that there were hundreds of temporary files in my system that needed to be purged for my computer to operate at a maximum level. After a few clicks of the mouse, I found myself preparing to empty the recycle bin. *(By now, I know that you can sense the metaphor com-ing.)*

Each of us has the innate ability to create the future with our thoughts, words and actions. What restrains individuals and organizations from operating at the optimal level in life, how-ever, are temporary files and leech files that no longer serve a purpose, but are saved to the hard-drive of your mind and spirit. These emotional gremlins require chunks of memory space, causing your computer processing unit, otherwise known as the heart of the system, to stall in executing. To move into a progressive future that awaits each one us, you must host a purging party to clean out the hard drive.

Ghost Files Will Haunt You

Ghost files are experiences from your past that haunt you and sometimes go "BOO" in the night. Let me share with you one of my ghost files.

In the summer of 2000, I was talking on the telephone with my mother on a typical Sunday night, which has been a tradition since I left home seventeen years ago. At the end of the discussion I asked if I could speak to my father. When Dad picked up the phone, we went through our usual greetings and small talk. Then out of nowhere, I said, "Dad why didn't you tell me when I was growing up that you loved me?" There was dead silence on the other end of the telephone line, as if he was collecting his thoughts, and finally he said, "Simon, I did love you." I shot back at him, saying, "But you never SAID IT." He took a deep breath and said, "I provided food for you. I put clothes on your back, and provided a roof over your head. I even taught you how to drive, and how to beat up the playground bully! There were many times that I did things for you that you can't even remember because you were too young."

I paused and took a deep breath and said, "But Daddy I needed to hear you say to me face to face that you loved me and you never did. Why didn't you say it?" My dad shared a story with me that has forever shifted my paradigm and brought me to the brink of tears on several occasions. When he was eight years of age, growing up in Kingston, Jamaica, his father passed away. Dad had to drop out of school to take care of the entire family of five. He would arise every morning at 4:30 A.M. to milk the cows and to complete other activities to produce meager means for the family to live on. Then he said, "Simon, I never told you that I loved you because there was no man in my life to tell me and to model for me what love, affection and affirmation was truly like."

You cannot give what you have not been given; you cannot do what has never been done; and you cannot be what you have never become." In other words, the fruit doesn't fall too far from the tree. Then he said the words that I wanted to hear all of my life, "Simon, I love you and believe in you." Seventeen years have since passed. Now I am embracing my four-year-old son and telling him that I love him. There is an internal struggle as I searched the file system of my heart to find the articulation to authentically communicate to him three simple words: I love you.

Heart File

Well, up until that time, I had created an internal file folder labeled "Searching for Daddy's Love." To hear the words of my father moved me in such a deep way, I had to dump the file from my system. Little did I know that my own fears, doubts and broken promises could cease to exist as the result of hearing my father's voice. All of my life, the only thing that I wanted to hear was that the man whose loins that I came out of was proud of me and that I was okay.

Every child wants to please his or her parents, and be the apple of a parent's eye. The positive emotional infrastructure in the early years of a child's development is cultivated any-where from eighteen months to five years. The heart of a child is like a sponge soaking up every emotional experience, and stores it for the rest of his or her life. Is it amazing to me what the mind and heart can recall at the most peculiar times? Of course it is! Somewhere deep within the base-ment of my soul was a longing for clarity of purpose and to know that my father was pleased with the person that I had become.

What is stored in your heart? What emotions run through your mind when you reflect on your past and current state of being? Do you believe that you have a bright future in front of you? I realized that my father did the best that he could with what he had. It was now my responsibility to forgive him and to enjoy the rest of our time here on Earth.

Unfinished Business

In many ways my job was my life. My boss and my superiors were like my parents, who always had a ton of rules and restrictions. My entire identity was wrapped up in my position, title, salary, corporate expense account, and cross-country travel. Little did I know that my boss was not equipped to play the role of a surrogate father. I was looking for love in all the wrong places, and searching for affirmation in all the wrong faces. I became numb to the aching pain of my heart, and brushed off the little inclinations that said it was time to go because my bills spoke louder than my dreams.

Today, you are in transition. Emotionally there is a hunger for your future to manifest instantly. Nevertheless, good things come to those who, through patience and virtue, understand the internal wrestling of emotional freedom. It was when I addressed my unfinished business and stopped beating myself up, for what I thought was a lack of parental love, that everything started to fall into place. Then I was able to tell my son that I loved him. My wife discovered the real man that she married, and I rediscovered the most incredible woman in the world who said, "I still do."

Once I understood that my emotions would run the rest of my life, I then began to evaluate personal and professional relationships, past decisions, hidden motives, and existing thinking. As a result of purging my system from the pain and disappointment of the past, I was able to install new mental models of thinking and believing into my current database. What about you? It's time to purge your system, reboot your life, and open the database of your life to infinite possibilities. It's time to free yourself. You will need to confront the factors that have harmed your spirit: confront people about issues, revisit places in person or in pictures, and list lessons learned from negative experiences. This is one of the most important things that you can do if you plan to live a passionate life.

Forgive yourself and move on. Whatever has happened is water under the bridge and there is no need to relive the pain of the past. I have lived with pain from my past. I have processed my issues through a bucket of tears and life coaching from Dr. Mark Chironna. I am a new man and I like the new me. The old me was horrible, negative and racist. Once I forgave myself, I was then able to move on and begin to fulfill my destiny. Remember to practice forgiveness and understanding, beginning with yourself.

Try these *Simon Says* to "Reboot Your Life."

Simon Says:

- Identify areas that you feel you may need improvement, and identify any dilemmas or issues you are facing.

- Conduct an inventory of people, places and experiences.

- Label each as a file and group them in folders; link the people, places and experiences.

- Identify each folder as a positive and negative.

- Look for common denominators within the negative folder.

SIMON SAYS....DREAM

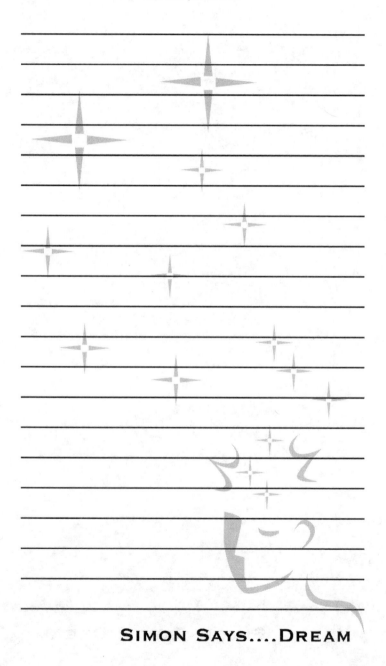

SIMON SAYS....DREAM

CHAPTER TEN

Simon Says...
"Follow your Heart Instead of Your Head!"

"Follow what you love to do. If you don't, you will probably backtrack later in your life to reclaim it anyway. My parents were shaped by the Depression. Their priorities stressed security, not the passionate pursuit of dreams. I was urged to become a teacher because it offered security. As I look back, the things that I loved when I was young were design and horticulture. Yet I wasn't sure enough of myself to pursue these until I was thirty-five. Don't make that mistake.

If you scratch the surface of what you don't love, you will find it empty and live the 'I wish I had.' But if you do what you love, you won't be able to get enough of it in a whole lifetime."

- Jacqueline Ignon

January 31, 2003, is a day that will go down in history for me. It was my last day as a full-time employee at one of the largest entertainment companies in the world. After almost seven years of enjoying an incredible pixie-dusted adventure, I decided that it was time for me to create my own magical moment. Many said, "Why are you leaving a great career, awesome benefits and a wonderful retirement plan? Why are you risking your family's security, especially with two young children? Why are you starting your own company in the middle of an economic recession, the ongoing threat of terrorism, pending war with Iraq, massive layoffs, and a time when Wall Street is predicting things will only get worse before they get better?"

Well, I decided to take the leap into the uncharted waters of entrepreneurship and navigate my way into the future. Why? I heard a small voice, deep within my heart, say, "It's time." Do you take risks or have you played it safe all of your life? Are you grateful for everything that you've learned thus far? Do you respect, appreciate and value every experience? Well, I am certainly grateful for all of the wonderful lessons that I learned, but I had to pursue what was most alive in me.

Have you ever heard a word, a phrase, a statement, or a whisper that came from within your innermost being? Was it so powerful and unusual that you had to look around to see if someone else was in the room talking to you? The reality is that nothing happens until you say it. Until you open your mouth and began to declare that something better is around the corner then you will be subjected to living out the vision of another person or organization. There is nothing wrong with fulfilling the dream of someone else. Working a job is fine. Earning a steady paycheck with benefits is a noble idea for every responsible human being on Earth. However, the question we have to ask ourselves is, "Are we fulfilled by what we do, who we've become, and what we've produced thus far?" Frederick Buechner says, we are in constant danger of being not actors in the drama of our lives, but reactors who "go where the world takes us, to drift with whatever current happens to be running the strongest." As for me, I was no longer fulfilled, satisfied or happy with the direction of my professional career. There was no one to blame but myself.

Transition Time

December 31, 2002—6:15 A.M. For most of my life I was trying to fulfill the needs of the world, meanwhile denying myself from living, being and doing the dreams of my heart. It was on this day that something erupted in my spirit and I knew that a season of change was about to happen. Was I afraid? Yes. Was I losing my mind? Perhaps, but I realized that to transition and enjoy a new frontier the voices of reason and analyticity had to yield to the peace that comforted my questioning mind and calmed my greatest fears. It was time for me to come alive and stop living down in the basement of limited thinking. The hour had come for me to twist the knob of reality and push open the door of opportunity, allowing me to ascend the stairs of potential.

The Moment of Truth

At first, I didn't say anything to my best friend, partner-in-all-things, lover, and mother of my children (all these roles found in one incredible person— my wife Reneé). To me, this was a chance to really see if she was my soul mate. This was the litmus test to discover if we were really spiritually connected after being married for more than a decade, with two children, a mortgage, and a grand dream that was taller than the Empire State building. I felt a movement in my soul like never before. My internal atmosphere was adjusting to the new climate of possibility that was emerging from the womb of my spirit. Playing small, thinking little, and generating no buzz was sifting the emotional energy of my heart. I had reached a place in my professional journey where I was stuck in neutral and going nowhere fast. The beat of my heart was pounding harder and harder as I reflected on King Mufasa's words to Simba: *"Remember who you are. "You are more than what you've become."* My mind was telling me, however, to play it safe, to not rock the boat.

I firmly believe that if you are not happy in your current place of employment, then find your happiness elsewhere. Every person who has ever founded a company or established an organization has the right to recruit and retain individuals who are committed to building a first-class operation. When a company is unable to strategically position human capital in a right-fit role, however, then that individual has the right to fire his or her company. A corporation is only profitable to the degree that human capital appreciates. The value of human capital depreciates over time when it is placed in a foreign land that does not leverage its core assets.

One day, my wife, without any prompting, said to me that she is with me no matter what I decide to do. Little did she know that I had asked God to speak to my wife and confirm through her what I already intuitively knew in my heart. At that time, I was entertaining three job offers, a potential internal transfer to another role with my then-current employer, and I still had a burning passion to communicate the words of life to the nations of the world. The moment of truth came when I said yes to my destiny. Have you experienced a moment of truth when you knew that something had to change for the better? What did you do? Are you still waiting for someone to tap you on the shoulder and show you the path to follow to live a life of fulfillment?

The Future is Waiting to be Created

On February 1, 2003, I started creating my future by taking a huge step in the direction of my heart's desire. Risky? Yes. Adventuresome? Of course. This day I affirmed out loud that this was the greatest day of my life and I am finally free to be authentically me. It felt so good to speak with clarity about what I believed in my heart. I had finally committed to being an active participant in the unfolding creative order of destiny. The process of self discovery had taken place in my mind. My heart was full of faith and hope, and my wife was my biggest fan. What more could a man need? I created the Imagination Institute to unleash human excellence in individuals and organizations from around the world.

Use these *Simon Says* to learn to follow your heart and not your head!

Simon Says:

- List things that you do well.

- List your dreams and aspirations. If you have difficulty identifying your dreams, then list all activities that make you happy or bring you pleasure.

- Associate career or entrepreneurial opportunities that could be sought via each or a combination of each.

- For each opportunity defined, perform an internal risk assessment, listing the pros and cons of each. Ask yourself, "Is it worth it?"

- Rank all opportunities for which you answered yes.

- Develop a plan for the opportunity with the highest ranking.

- Pray!

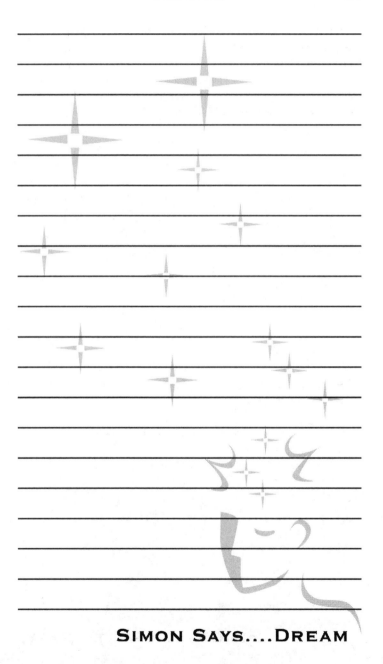

SIMON SAYS....DREAM

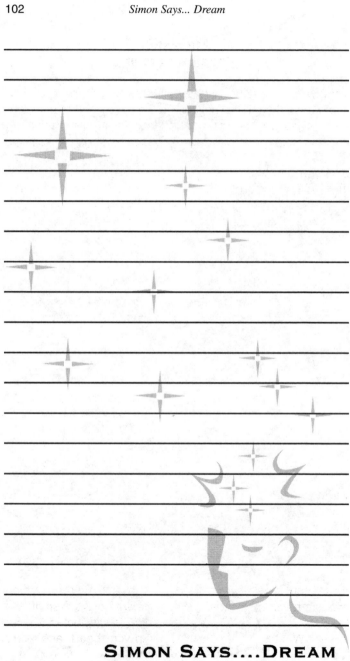

SIMON SAYS....DREAM

Afterword
Inspire Yourself

The future is created every day and is shaped by our thinking, our words and our actions. To create a world of unlimited
possibilities, we must begin to shape the future by filtering
our thoughts, upgrading our language and acting on what
you see in your mind's eye. Nothing will come into existence
until you use words that carry you in the direction of your
heart's desire. Our thoughts create words, which lead to
action, which then cause us to live in the present. Francisco
Varela, a distinguished professor of cognitive science and
epistemology at École Polytechnique and the Institute of
Neuroscience in Paris, said this: "Our language and our nervous system combine to constantly construct our environment. We can only see what we talk about, because we are
speaking 'blind,' beyond language. Language is like another
set of eyes and hands for the nervous system, through which
we coordinate actions with others. We lay it down as we walk
on its path." We can describe the world we see, but we should
also see the world we describe.

God almighty, the creator of the universe, spoke this world
into existence, and then created man in his image and after
his likeness. Creativity and excellence are two trademarks to
describe the maker of heaven and earth! This means the
ability to create a fulfilled life, in the spirit of excellence, exists
in every human being! Nothing changes until you decide that
you are ready to change. Suddenly you will feel inspired to
make a decision, attend a meeting in pursuit of what is most
alive in you, and tell yourself that your better days are ahead
of you, no matter how old you are. Just remember that you
are like a fine wine—you only get better with time!

Adjust your mental photography and see the New You. When
you listen with your heart, within the well of your spirit, the
truth will make you free! Your freedom is connected to your
vision. What you see is saved within your heart, and every

time you seek inspiration, suddenly you begin to repeat the desire of your heart. Inspire yourself. Review your progress. Celebrate your results, and treat yourself to an ice cream sundae!

I am inviting you to go for it and to follow your heart, not your head!

About the Author
Simon T. Bailey, MA

Simon T. Bailey is chief creative officer of the human development company, Imagination Institute, Inc. based in Orlando, Florida. "Engaging," "thought-provoking" and "passionate" are the words to describe Simon, who is one of the most sought-after speakers in America today. Recently, he delivered an inspiring commencement address to ten-thousand people at Florida A&M University. Former featured speakers at this event have included such notable personalities as Bill Cosby and Madeleine Albright. Charging, changing and challenging the spirit and minds of individuals to make their lives, organizations, companies, and ultimately their societies a better, more productive place is Simon's mission. He accomplishes this by serving as a business speaker, consultant and life coach.

Bailey has received rave reviews for his candid, charismatic, yet practical, approach to building the world's most valuable resource, its people. He has been featured in the *Omaha World Herald* (Omaha, Nebraska) for his moving keynote address to the National Urban League. The *Buffalo Evening News* (Buffalo, New York) featured excerpts from his keynote presentation to the community's leaders and entrepreneurs.

Simon was nominated for Central Florida's "Top Business and Community Leader" and was selected by the Leukemia Society as its 2000 Central Florida "Man of the Year." *Florida Trend* business magazine did a full-page feature story on Simon and selected him as its 2002 Trendsetter. In 2003 the city of Miami presented him with the key to the city and recognized him as a distinguished visitor.

Simon's professional career started with Hyatt Hotels and Resorts where he was selected "Manager of the Year." As a result of his success, he joined the Orlando Convention and Visitors Bureau, where he served as national account manager, responsible for promoting the city of Orlando to international associations, multinational corporations, and global incentives companies.

Success and accomplishments at a national level set the foundation for Simon to be pursued by the world's number one entertainment conglomerate, the Walt Disney Company. He joined Disney in 1996 as senior sales manager. While there, Premier Convention Services honored him as its "Supplier of the Year." Simon progressed and was promoted swiftly through the Disney organization. In 1998, he was elevated to director of sales for the Resort Sales division. He led the team that handled all group travel contracts for countries in Latin America, Asia-Pacific and Europe. As a result of his success in resort sales, he joined Disney Institute as a customized program consultant. During his tenure, he designed and delivered programs to groups at Disneyland Paris and Walt Disney World Resort® in Florida. Prior to leaving Disney in 2003, he was the new business development director/sales director for Disney Institute, where he engineered the sales effort for Fortune 500 companies and organizations worldwide.

A native of Buffalo, New York, Simon graduated magna cum laude from Life Christian University, where he earned a bachelor's degree in theology. He graduated summa cum laude from Faith Christian University in Orlando, Florida where he earned a master of arts degree in theology. He is also a graduate of the Rollins College Executive Management Program. He serves on board of directors for the Greater Orlando Leadership Foundation. On this board, the key mission is to identify other future community leaders. He also serves on the board of trustees for the Orlando Marine Institute and Florida Men of Integrity.

Stay Connected

Simon's inspirational, leading-edge, and knowledge-packed presentations, seminars and workshops will have you and your participants applying the information he provides immediately and successfully!

To learn more about all the exciting programs Simon has to offer:

Call (407) 877-9386 * Fax (407) 877-0939
or
Send email to info@simonsaysdream.com.

Be sure to sign up for Simon's weekly,
"30-Second Inspirational Tip" by visiting his Web site at
www.simonsaysdream.com.

To order additional copies of this book:
Please visit www.IPpublishingOnline.com or contact:
Infinite Possibilities Publishing Group, Inc.
PO Box 150823
Altamonte Springs, FL 32715-0823
(407) 699-6603 SE Division * (917) 842-9498 NE Division

Overcoming the World, One Verse at a Time...